CW01651487

action science

WILLIAM MERRICK
JOAN O'SULLIVAN

THE ENVIRONMENT

Oxford University Press, Walton Street, Oxford OX2 6DP

Oxford New York Toronto
Delhi Bombay Calcutta Madras Karachi
Petaling Jaya Singapore Hong Kong Tokyo
Nairobi Dar es Salaam Cape Town
Melbourne Auckland

and associated companies in
Berlin Ibadan

Oxford is a trade mark of Oxford University Press

ISBN 0 19 914320 X

Typeset in Century Old Style & Helvetica Light Italic
Pentacor PLC, High Wycombe, Bucks
Printed in Hong Kong

First published 1990

WRITING TEAM

David Appleby, Biddenham Upper School, Bedford
Alan Jarvis, Inspector, Bedfordshire LEA
William Merrick, Challney High School, Luton
Joan O'Sullivan, Putteridge High School, Luton
Pam Slade, Science Advisor, Redbridge

To my wife Judith and my daughters Angela and Lucy. (WM)

I wish to thank my husband Eugene for all his help in producing this book. (JO'S)

We wish to thank Oxford University Press for their confidence in us and for their valuable contributions and help at all stages of production.

ACKNOWLEDGEMENTS

Aga-Rayburn: p 31 (right); Animal Aid: p 25; Barnaby's Picture Library: pp 4, 18, 24, 33; BASF PLC: p 11; Heather Angel/Biofotos: p 6 (left); J Allan Cash: pp 19, 34 (bottom right), 45 (centre right), 45 (centre); Holt Studios: pp 24, 33 (right), 36, 41; Oxfam: p 42; Oxford Scientific Films: pp 5, 6 (right), 7 (bottom, top), 9 (top, centre), 16 (right, left), 17 (all), 29, 31 (left), 33, 38, 45 (top, top right, top left, bottom left, bottom centre, bottom right, centre left); Science Photo Library: p 33 (bottom right); Spectrum: p 37; Zefa Photographic Library: p 40.

Additional photography by Marilyn O'Brien. Illustrations by Oena Armstrong, Susannah English, Gordon Hendry, Rachel Lockwood, Julie Tolliday and Galina Zolfaghari. Cover illustration by Paul Hunt.

The authors wish to thank: OXFAM; CAFOD; Band Aid Trust; Lynx; The Canadian Embassy; The International Fund For Animal Welfare; Greenpeace; The Nature Conservancy Council; Data Support for Education (Simon Albrecht); The Wildfowl Trust, Slimbridge; Care Of The Wild, Horsham; RSPB, Sandy; Worldwide Fund for Nature, Godalming.

CONTENTS

Plant homes pages 4–11

Discover why different plants grow in different places
Learn about the conditions affecting the growth of plants
Argue the cases for and against ploughing wet meadows
Design a plant to grow in a particular habitat
Analyse data on the results of tomato growth

Chains and webs pages 12–19

Learn about food chains and food webs
Find out what keeps the numbers in a population steady
Discover what is causing the decrease in barn-owl numbers
Write an account of how to maintain a stable population of elephants
Analyse data obtained from small animals collected in a pitfall trap
Suggest reasons to explain the disappearance of fish from a pond

How do plants get their food? pages 20–27

Compare a sugar factory with a leaf
Discover how plants get their food
Learn about pyramids of numbers, mass, and energy
Find out about factory farming
Calculate which animals make most protein

Keeping a balance pages 28–35

Find out how plants and animals depend on each other
Discover why dead things decay
Learn about the cycles that exist in nature
Construct a nitrogen cycle
Produce a report on the greenhouse effect

Case studies pages 36–43

Discover why the seal is in danger
Research the history of DDT
Find out how golden eagle numbers have changed
Consider the causes of famine in Ethiopia

Data pages pages 44–45

Crops and climate
World environments

Extension activities pages 46, 47

Describe the seasonal variation for certain places
Choose suitable crops for growing in these areas
Suggest ways in which land can be improved for growing crops
Argue the cases for and against cutting down tropical rain forests

Index page 48

ASHWOOD IN SUMMER

These two woodlands have very different plants growing in them. The pie charts show the distributions of plants of the undergrowth for the two different woodlands.

A *Use the pie charts to list the differences between the two woodland environments. Give reasons to suggest why they are different.*

BEECHWOOD IN SUMMER

B *We have many different trees in our woodlands, for example oak, ash and beech. Why are woodlands not all the same type?*

C *Why are there no bluebells to be seen in this picture?*

FACTFILE

PLANT HOMES

A SUITABLE LOCATION

The plants that you see growing around you are of many different kinds. If you visit other parts of the world you will find even more variety. All plants are adapted to their own range of conditions which they need for healthy growth. The temperature, amount of light and rain, the type of soil and the nutrients available will all affect the plants that can grow in a habitat. Farmers may change the conditions to grow the plants that we need.

TEMPERATURE

Every type of plant is adapted to a particular range of temperatures at which it will grow best. Plants will die if the temperature goes too high or too low.

Alpines survive by dying back in the winter. The underground bulb remains to continue growth next spring

The prickly pear thrives in hot, dry places but cannot survive snow, ice and frost

SOIL pH

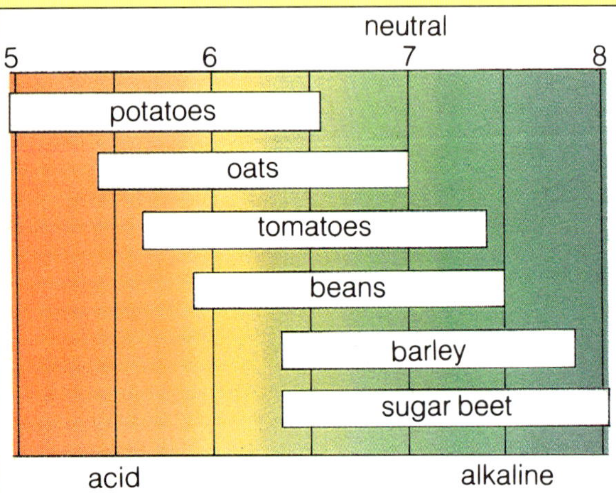

Plants like **heathers** *and* **rhododendrons** *grow in acid soils, e.g. heathland. Other plants like* **old man's beard** *and many* **orchids** *prefer alkaline conditions, such as chalk downland.*

LIGHT LEVELS

Green plants cannot grow without light. Plants such as **dog's mercury** *and* **bluebells** *are found in dark woodlands where only a little light penetrates. This ability to grow with little light means these plants are not overshadowed by faster growing plants which need more light.*

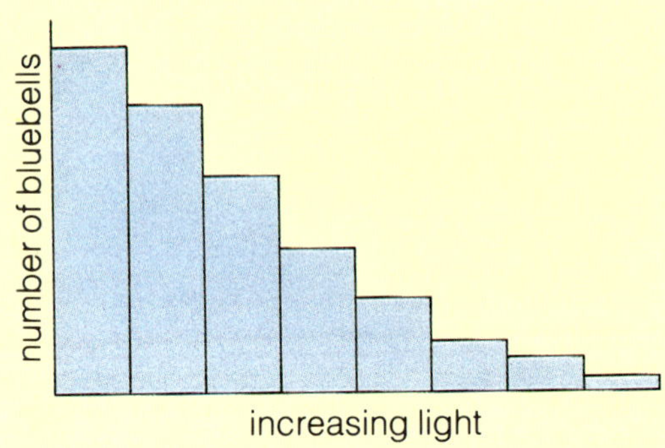

NUTRIENTS

Minerals or nutrients are needed for plants to grow. They are absorbed by the roots of plants.

nutrient	symbol	absorbed as
nitrogen	N	nitrates
phosphorus	P	phosphates
potassium	K	potassium ions

Nitrates are needed to make protein. The plant **clover** *is adapted to live in soil low in nitrates. If a soil is low in minerals, a farmer will have to add fertilizers for the crops to grow.*

SOIL TEXTURE

The texture of the soil depends on the size of the mineral particles. The texture determines the amount of water held by the soil and its drainage properties.

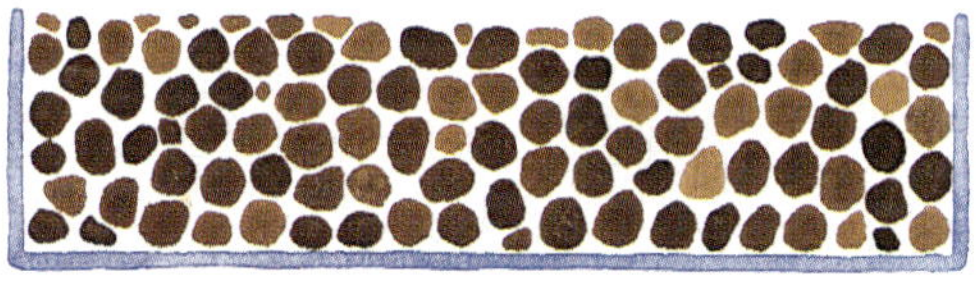

Light soils *are made of larger mineral particles giving it a sandy texture, plenty of air and good drainage.*

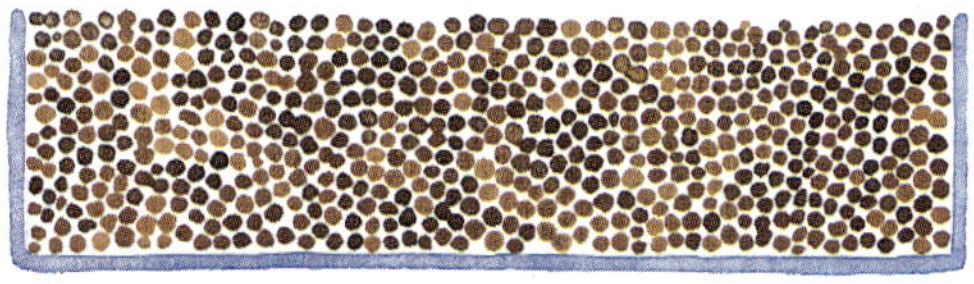

Heavy soils *are made up of very fine clay particles which become sticky and difficult to dig when wet. Heavy soils contain little air and the drainage is poor.*

WATER AND DRAINAGE

Plant roots need oxygen and without it they will die. This is why soil saturated with water kills most plants. Other plants have roots which are able to grow with less available oxygen. These are found in ponds, lakes, fens, marshes and other aquatic sites.

Marsh plants are suited to living in or by water

Sand-dune grasses have long roots to find water

MARSHES AND MEADOWS

In the past, farming has encouraged the development of damp grasslands rich in wild flowers. These meadows were used for grazing and hay-making. Grazing cattle drop dung and urine onto the fields releasing the nutrients nitrogen and phosphorus into the soil. As long as over-grazing is avoided, a balance will be achieved and no extra fertilizers will be needed. Where the grassland is next to water, it may be flooded from time to time. If the soil is constantly waterlogged it becomes a marsh.

Wildlife of wet meadows

Wetland communities

These damp grasslands have different communities of plants and animals depending on the amount of soil moisture and the type of grazing. Many of the plants have beautiful flowers but unfortunately some of them are now becoming rare. Damp grasslands are also home for butterflies, dragonflies, frogs, toads, newts, reptiles, birds and some mammals. Grasslands have been managed for many years and the wildlife is there because of human activities. Changes in these practices now threaten these rich communities.

Where have all the flowers gone?

Much of our damp grassland has now been destroyed. Ploughing of old meadows, reseeding with rye grass or crops, and drainage have caused dramatic changes in the plant populations. It's not just the plants which suffer; once the habitat has been lost, all the animals die too.

The nitrate problem

Increasing concern has been expressed at the problems facing many of the freshwater sites in this country. Nitrates from fertilizers are washed off the fields into rivers and ponds. These extra minerals in the water cause algae to grow rapidly. They form a layer across the surface of the water blocking out the light and preventing the growth of larger water plants. In time, as the algae decay, the oxygen in the water is used up resulting in the death of most of the wildlife.

A *Read the magazine article on page 9. Write a letter from Mr Marshal to the local council giving his reasons for ploughing the land. He will need to explain how this will benefit the area.*

B *Write a report from the local conservation group to the local council giving reasons for keeping 'Greenfields' hay meadow.*

C *Look at the advertisement in the* Grower's Gazette. *Can you spot a false claim? Why is it false?*

GREENFIELDS

'Greenfields' is a small area of hay meadow of a type which has become rare in lowland Britain through farming improvement. The outstanding features of this site are the large populations of the **green-winged orchid**, **the wild daffodil** and **the fritillary**. The stretch of the river alongside the meadow is known to be part of the feeding territory of an otter. The owner, Mr Marshal, intends to plough, fertilize and reseed the meadow with **rye grass**. He wishes to improve the grazing for his cattle. The local council are holding a public enquiry to decide whether or not Mr Marshal should be allowed to make these changes.

Grower's Gazette

POOR GRAZING?

Use GROWOL to improve plant growth.

For best results plough, fertilize, and seed with quick-growing rye grass.

Alternatively you could get rid of those unwanted plants with KILLOL.

Simply mix to the right strength, spray, wait three months and reseed with rye grass.

GROWOL and KILLOL the complete solution!

Questions and Activities

A *Why do plant shapes differ?*

Plants look different because their shapes have become suited to the different habitats in which they grow. Some plants have very small needle-like leaves so that they lose very little water from the leaf surfaces and avoid damage by strong winds. Plants that live in very dry places need long, spreading roots to search for water.

Where do these plants grow? Match the letter by each plant to one of the habitats. One example has been filled in already. Copy out the chart and fill in the letter and reason for your choice. The **factfile** may help you.

habitat	plant	reason for choice
wall	F	roots along the stem grip the wall
river – fast flowing water		
pond – stagnant water		
sand-dune – high winds, average rainfall, good drainage		
desert – hot, dry winds		
chalk downland – dry grazed by sheep		

B *Design a plant*

Design the type of plant you think would be most suited to live in each of the three places described on the right. Make a large diagram of each of your plants and label those features which would help it to live in the habitat. Think about the right kind of root, stem and leaf.

- On rocks at the sea-shore, pounded by waves.
- In the middle of a pond where the water level is likely to rise and fall.
- High up, near the top of a mountain.

c *Growth of tomato plants*

Tomato growing has become very popular in this country. Best results are obtained when they are grown in a heated greenhouse. The fruit is of better quality and matures much earlier than from outdoor planting. In the greenhouse the crop may still be available when all outside sources of supply have been cut down by frost. The yield of tomatoes from a greenhouse is higher than from a similar number of plants outside. The increased temperature of the greenhouse means that tomatoes are able to grow at a faster rate. Light intensity is also important. Tomatoes grown in shady places produce low yields while those under bright lights are able to produce more fruit per plant.

The table opposite shows some results of growing tomatoes at different temperatures for low and high light levels. Yield is expressed as kg per plant.

	yield per plant	
day temperature	low light	high light
12°C	0.9kg	0.9kg
15°C	1.3kg	1.4kg
18°C	3.5kg	5.5kg
21°C	3.6kg	8.7kg
24°C	3.4kg	7.7kg
27°C	2.7kg	6.5kg

- Why are tomatoes usually grown under glass?
- What other conditions, in addition to light and temperature, affect the yields of tomatoes? The **factfile** may help you.
- Look at the data for tomato yields. Plot a graph of yield against temperature for the two light levels.
- What conditions will give the highest yields?
- What yield would you expect if you grew the plants at 20°C under (a) a low light level, and (b) a high light level?
- Why does the light level not make any difference to yield at 12°C?
- Why do you think there was hardly any change in yield between 18°C and 24°C when the plants were grown at low light levels?

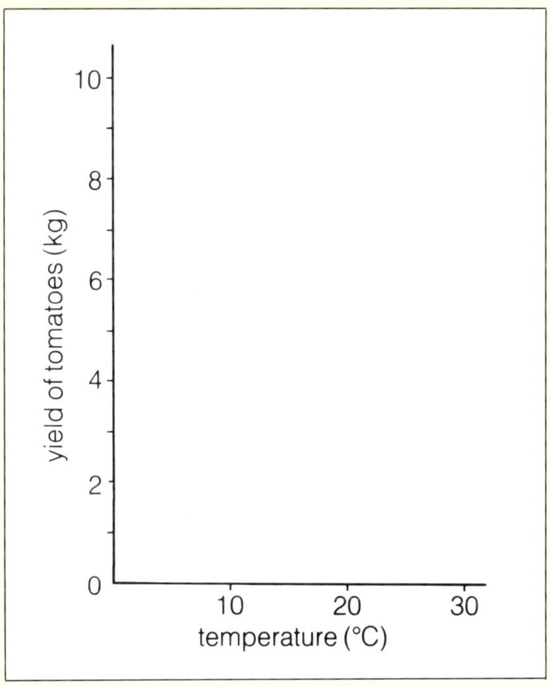

A FOOD CHAIN IN ACTION

A butterfly feeds on nectar from a flower

A dragonfly captures the butterfly

A frog captures the dragonfly

A snake makes a meal of the frog

The hawk lands on its prey

The hawk flies off with the snake

A *Construct a food chain which starts with nectar and ends with a hawk. The* **factfile** *might help you.*

B *Construct another food chain which ends with you. Put in as many links as possible.*

COMMUNITY LIFE

A *Ponds always contain lots of animals. They all need to eat. If the animals at the top of the food chain eat the animals in the pond, how can the pond continue to be so full of life?*

B *Choose one of the animals shown above. Find out as much as you can about it, especially what it eats.*

FACTFILE

CHAINS AND WEBS

FOOD CHAINS

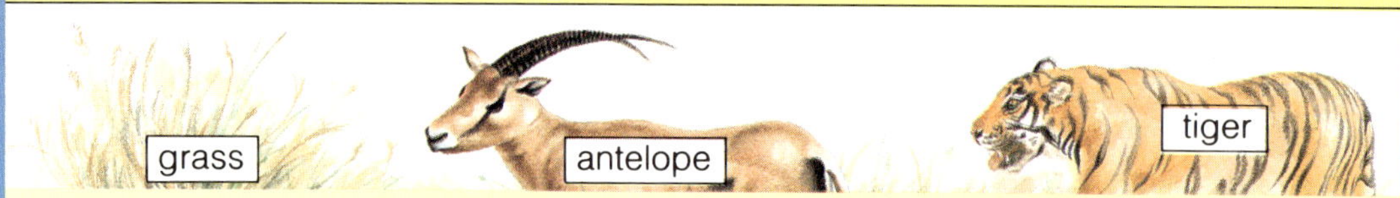

The food chain shows energy flowing from plants to herbivores to carnivores. Each arrow means **is eaten by**. *It shows the direction of the energy flow. The food chain can be as short as just three different organisms.*

LETTUCE → RABBIT → FOX

Sometimes they are longer.

GRASS → GRASSHOPPER → TOAD → HAWK

ROSE → GREENFLY → LADYBIRD → SPIDER → THRUSH

LIMITING FACTORS

As a population grows, we usually find that it increases rapidly for a time and then levels off.

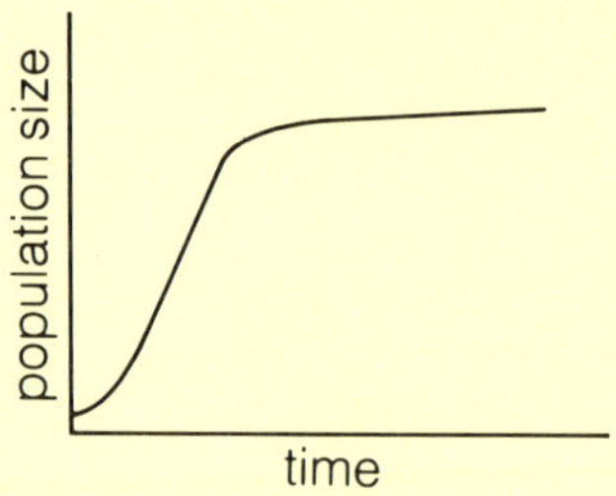

It may stop increasing due to insufficient food, space or too many predators. Some factor always limits the size of the population.

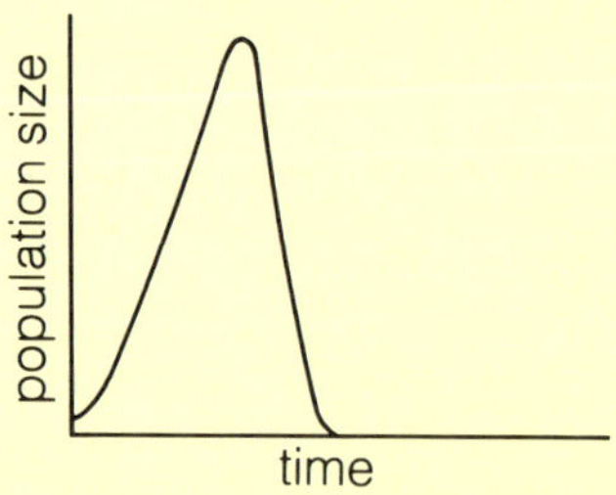

When there is no factor to limit the size of a population, then the numbers will increase rapidly. Where this has happened it can result in the animals destroying their own habitat. An example of this is African elephants in game parks (see page 19). Eventually the whole population will collapse resulting in an ecological disaster.

FINDING OUT THE NUMBERS IN A POPULATION

Usually there are too many animals in a habitat to count them all. We have to count how many there are in a small part. This is called taking a **sample**. *Most animals move about so we have to trap them. These traps will not harm the animals.*

Pitfall traps *can be used to collect small animals such as woodlice, earwigs, beetles, millipedes and centipedes. The trap is emptied each day. The animals are then counted and released. We could set these traps up in different places to find out how the numbers of animals vary with the different habitats.*

FOOD WEBS

Usually an animal eats several different types of plants, not just one. A carnivore hunts for several different kinds of herbivores. These can be shown in a **food web**. *It is more complicated than a food chain but it is really the same idea. It still shows the flow of energy from the plants, through the herbivores and into the carnivores.*

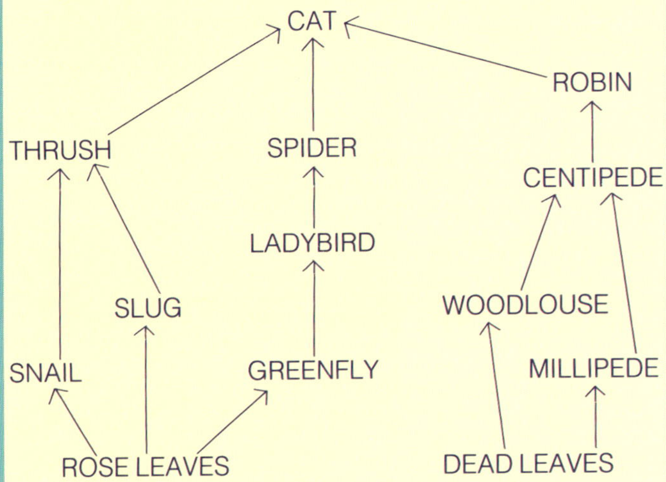

WORD WISE

Species — *Animals or plants of the same kind which are able to breed with each other.*

Population — *The number of organisms of one kind in a particular place.*

Community — *A group of animals and plants living in the same habitat.*

Habitat — *The place where the animals and plants live.*

Herbivore — *An animal which feeds on plants.*

Carnivore — *An animal which feeds on other animals.*

Omnivore — *An animal which feeds on plants and animals.*

Predator — *An animal which hunts and feeds on other animals.*

WHAT KEEPS THE NUMBERS IN A POPULATION STEADY?

how much food there is

competition for food and space

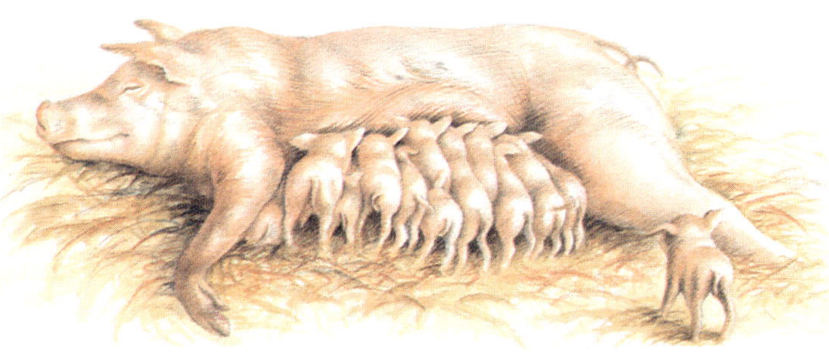

disease

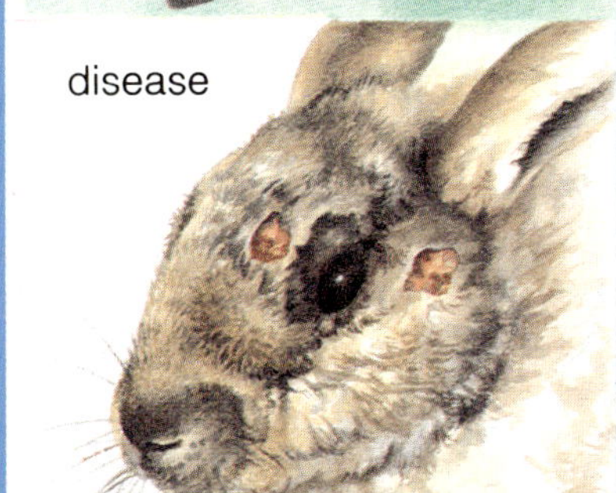

number of predators

seasonal change

WHERE HAVE ALL THE BARN-OWLS GONE?

The barn-owl, once a common bird of our countryside, is now becoming one of our rarest breeding birds. The numbers have more than halved in the last fifty years and they are still decreasing.

Where is it found?

The barn-owl lives in most parts of Europe except Scandinavia. It prefers the warmer climate of the Mediterranean although it does live in the colder, northern regions. The barn-owl needs a suitable nest site close to a good hunting area usually within a distance of 1km. Nest sites vary from ruins to holes in cliffs and trees but old farm buildings are the barn-owl's favourite site.

A barn-owl returns with food for its young

What does it eat?

The barn-owl feeds mainly on small mammals like voles, shrews and mice. It also eats small birds and occasionally insects. All the prey are caught alive. When the barn-owl has young to feed it takes the prey back to the nest. This encourages the owlets to recognize which animals to catch when they are old enough to hunt.

Breeding

Courtship begins in March and the male brings food to the female every day. Egg-laying occurs in late April and May and between four and seven eggs are laid; the average is 4.9. The eggs are incubated for about 33 days and the average number of young is 3.0. The young owlets are able to fly after about ten weeks.

Young barn-owls in South Devon

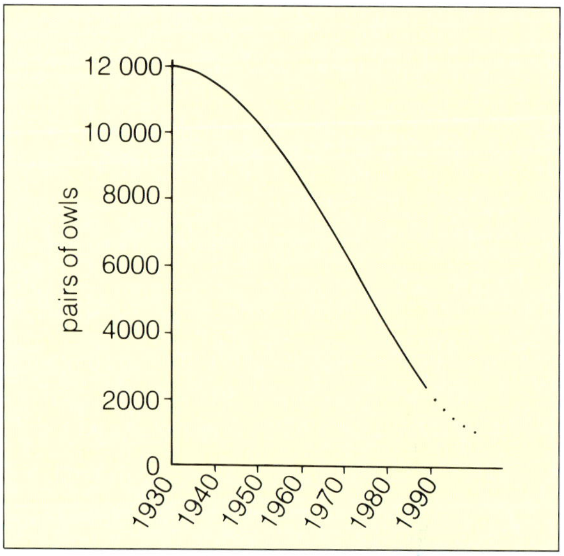

Numbers of barn-owls, 1930–1990

Why are the numbers decreasing?

Snow cover One of the most important factors affecting the number of barn-owls is the amount of snow cover. Most snow falls between January and March. For birds to breed successfully an ample food supply is important during these months. When the ground is covered with snow, finding small mammals becomes more difficult and can have serious affects on the numbers of young owls reared.

The bank vole makes up a large part of the owl's diet

Heavy rainfall Barn-owls have little wax on their feathers. In heavy rain they become waterlogged and cannot fly. Their young can die of starvation if rain continues for too long.

Drought Summer drought reduces growth of grass and therefore the numbers of voles. This again can affect the numbers of barn-owls.

Loss of habitat As the countryside is changed, fewer places are available for small mammals to feed and breed. Possible nesting sites may be destroyed as farm buildings are changed and fewer old trees are left.

The tawny-owl in the snow

Competition with the tawny-owl The tawny-owl appears to be less bothered by disturbance. The numbers have been increasing and competing for available food with the barn-owl.

Pesticides New pesticides have been introduced to destroy rats and mice. These chemicals are now known to be harmful to owls.

Changes in hay storage The old haystacks used to house large numbers of small mammals. This was a good source of food for the barn-owls during the winter months. Different ways of storing food have meant that this supply of mammals is no longer available.

Road deaths The strips of grass alongside roads are important breeding areas for many small mammals. Barn-owls are attracted to these places to hunt. Unfortunately many owls are killed by vehicles.

A *Copy out the food chains below and fill in the spaces.*

GRASS → ? → BARN-OWL

? → ? → TAWNY-OWL

Using all the information on the barn-owl, make up a food web including as many animals and plants as you can.

B *What would you expect to happen to the numbers of barn-owls if:*

- *there was a large increase in the numbers of tawny-owls;*
- *a new pesticide was used to kill the small mammals?*

C *Mr Titus Oats has a large farm growing cereal crops and keeping dairy cattle. He was delighted to find he had a pair of barn-owls nesting in his barn. Suggest ways in which he could help to ensure their survival.*

Questions and Activities

A Look at the photograph of the animals at the water-hole. Copy out the paragraph below it and put the words in the right places.

herbivore, carnivore, habitat, community, population

The grasslands of Africa make up a ______ called the savannah. In it we find a huge ______ of zebra. A zebra eats only grass and other green plants, so it is a ______. The lion eats only meat, and is the largest ______ in Africa. The plants and animals all live together and depend on each other, so they make up a ______.

B In the last six pages you have learned about many different habitats. Draw a table like the one below, and make lists of the herbivores and carnivores in the habitats. Don't forget to check the pictures as well as the words.

	herbivore	carnivore
garden woodland pond savannah marsh		

C Look at the drawing of a pond on page 13. Construct a food web like the one in the **factfile**.

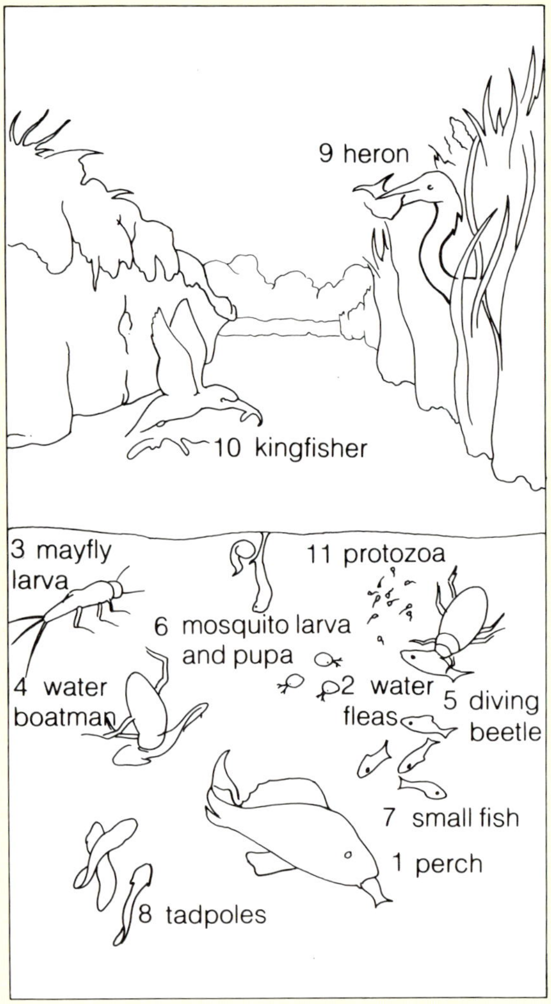

The facts listed below also have to fit in.

- Water fleas, mayfly larvae and gnat larvae eat microscopic plants and animals.
- When tadpoles first hatch they eat plants. Later on they eat tiny animals.
- Small fish feed on water fleas, mayfly larvae and gnat larvae.
- Perch eat water beetles and water boatmen.

D Pitfall traps were placed in four different places in a garden for ten days. Each morning they were emptied, the animals counted and returned to their surroundings.

- Choose a suitable method to display the figures in the table graphically.
- When are these animals likely to be active – day or night?
- From these results can you tell which animals are likely to be herbivores and which are carnivores? Give reasons for your choices.

habitat	centipedes	millipedes	woodlice	earwigs	beetles
under tree	5	15	32	17	12
in lawn	1	20	7	4	2
in undergrowth near pond	7	18	35	12	16
in vegetable garden	4	26	21	7	8

E *Bent on self destruction?*

African elephants have been hunted for their meat, as hunters' trophies and for their ivory tusks. As more land has been used for farming, their territories have become smaller and their numbers have decreased.

To avoid further losses, some African countries developed large game reserves where the elephants could be protected. The result was a dramatic increase in the numbers of elephants. This resulted in an unexpected tragedy. The elephants first ate all the available plants. Still hungry they began to remove the bark and branches of trees. After a time the land looked more like a desert and the elephants began to die of starvation.

What must the game-wardens do if they wish to maintain a population of elephants that the grassland can support?

F *Where have all the fish gone?*

Villagers at Little Tipping have become worried about their village pond. The pond used to have a large population of fish but for the last few months fewer fish have been spotted. Mr Cane has sat by the pond for a couple of hours every Sunday for the last twenty years. 'I used to throw in some bread and the whole surface was alive with fish fighting over the food. Now I am lucky if I see one fish.'

Our local wildlife expert, Jo Peters, said it could be due to a number of reasons. 'Perhaps predators are responsible or there may be too much decaying vegetation at the bottom of the pond. This would use up the available oxygen needed by the fish.'

Discuss in groups other possible reasons for the loss of fish in the pond. Make a list of the reasons that seem most likely.

THE SUGAR FACTORY

The illustration below is of an imaginary sugar factory. This represents the processes that occur within a green leaf.

SUNLIGHT TO SUGAR

Green plants usually have lots of leaves. Their purpose is to make food for the plant. This process is called **photosynthesis**.

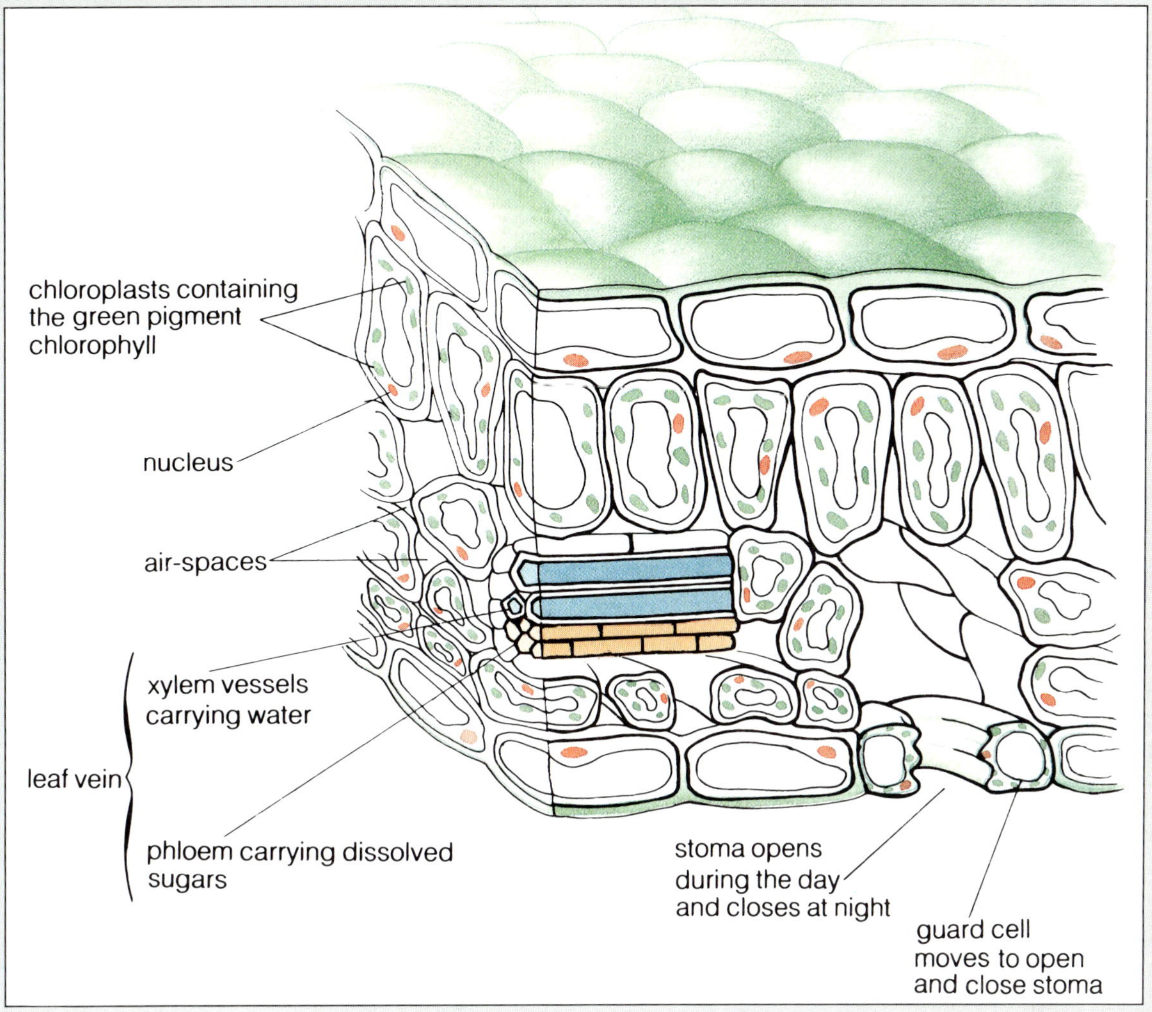

A *Study the drawing of the sugar factory and write a brief description of the process. Include a list of the raw materials, and describe the energy source, the waste produced and the end-products obtained.*

B *The factory opposite represents a green leaf and the process is photosynthesis. Work out how the chemicals involved enter and leave the leaf shown above and where photosynthesis takes place.*

C *Copy out the chart and fill in the information.*

stomata	*open to let ______ enter leaf and ______ pass out of leaf*
xylem	*carries ______ from root to leaf*
chlorophyll	*green colour which receives ______ energy*
chloroplasts	*site where ______ are made*
phloem	*carries ______ away from leaf to be used for growth and respiration*

FACTFILE

HOW DO PLANTS GET THEIR FOOD?

EXPERIMENTS CAN SHOW THAT LEAVES CARRY OUT PHOTOSYNTHESIS

Place leaf in boiling water to kill leaf and stop photosynthesis → Place leaf in boiling alcohol to remove the chlorophyll → Wash leaf in hot water to soften the leaf → Cover leaf in iodine solution to find out if starch is present

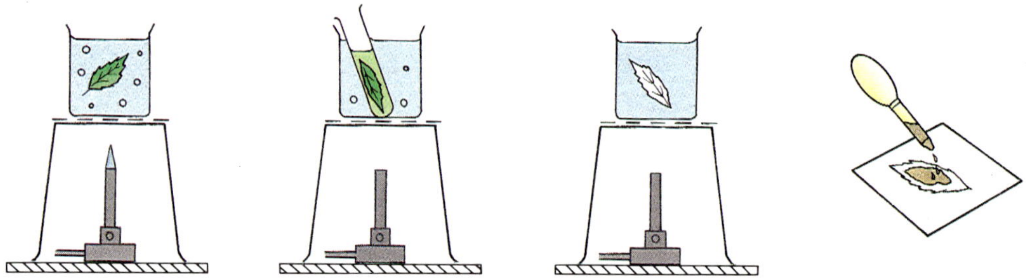

PHOTOSYNTHESIS

All living things need food for energy and growth. Plants can make their own food. Carbon dioxide and water combine to make sugars and release oxygen. The energy needed to make this happen comes from the sun. Light energy is absorbed by **chlorophyll**, *the green pigment in leaves. The sugars made in the leaf cannot be stored and so they are stored as starch.*

$$\text{water} + \text{carbon dioxide} \xrightarrow[\text{chlorophyll}]{\text{light}} \text{sugars} + \text{oxygen}$$

LEAF RESULT

brown leaf
no starch
no photosynthesis

blue/black leaf
starch present
photosynthesis carried out

WHERE DOES THE ENERGY FROM THE SUN END UP?

The glucose in leaves is used to make:

starch – *a food store which can be changed back to glucose when it is needed;*

cellulose – *the material which makes cell walls;*

protein – *glucose and mineral salts which combine to make plant proteins.*

THE ENERGY CHAIN

Energy is collected from the sun and used by living things for movement, warmth and growth. The sugar molecules made in photosynthesis are used by animals for their activities. Animals are running on solar power! Some of the energy in the food eaten by an animal:

- *is stored in its body chemicals as it grows;*
- *is used for moving about;*
- *is used for keeping warm (mammals and birds);*
- *is lost in its waste products;*
- *is lost as heat.*

PYRAMIDS OF NUMBERS, MASS AND ENERGY

The organisms that make up a food chain are arranged as a pyramid with the plants at the base, the herbivores next and the carnivores on the top. Because energy is lost at each stage in a food chain, the base of the pyramid will be greater than the top. You can draw pyramids of numbers, biomass (total dry mass) or energy.

Usually the shape will be a pyramid but there are exceptions. If a large number of herbivores are feeding on one plant, then the shape is different.

THE GREEN REVOLUTION

Plant breeders have developed new strains of cereals which grow more quickly and have much higher yields. These new strains need larger quantities of fertilizers and water. It was hoped that growing these crops would help to feed the world's population. Unfortunately there have been problems. Some of the new strains are more likely to suffer from diseases than older varieties and many of the developing nations are not able to buy the large quantities of fertilizers needed. These plants are not adapted to survive in countries suffering from droughts. In time, the plant breeders will be able to produce new strains more suited to the conditions existing in different countries.

The bigger the better?

Plant eaters or meat eaters?

Each meal in the illustration above was produced from 5 acres of land. As there is a 90% energy loss at each stage in a food chain it would make more sense if we all ate plants and not meat. We could feed far more people in the world because less energy would be lost.

Factory farming

We can increase the amount of plants used directly as food but there will still be a large number of people who want to eat meat. Factory farming involves keeping animals under conditions which convert more of the energy in their food into animal protein than if they had been raised in the fields. Hens, pigs and cows are kept in special buildings where maximum food production is the main priority.

Intensively-reared pigs

Battery hens

Hens are kept in battery cages for about one year while they are laying eggs. Often two to three chickens are kept in each cage, usually stacked three cages high. A conveyor belt runs under each layer of cages to collect their waste matter. Eggs laid by the birds run down a sloping floor so that they are easy to collect. Food is passed along in trays and a continuous water supply is piped to the cages.

Controlling the conditions

The environment in the house is controlled for temperature, ventilation and lighting. The reason for controlling the temperature is so that the bird uses less of its food to maintain a constant body temperature. Heat from the birds' bodies is used to heat the building. The walls and roof are well insulated to prevent heat escaping. Ventilators in the roof are controlled to increase or decrease the flow of fresh air.

Disadvantages of production

Keeping hens in batteries means that eggs can be produced and sold to people at a much lower cost but there are some disadvantages.

- The hens can become bored and peck each other or try to eat their eggs.
- When hens are kept so close together the spread of disease is more likely. Antibiotics may be given to control this but it may mean these chemicals are present in their eggs.
- Pesticides are sometimes sprayed onto the poultry to reduce the spread of mites and lice.
- Many people regard keeping animals in such confined spaces as cruel.

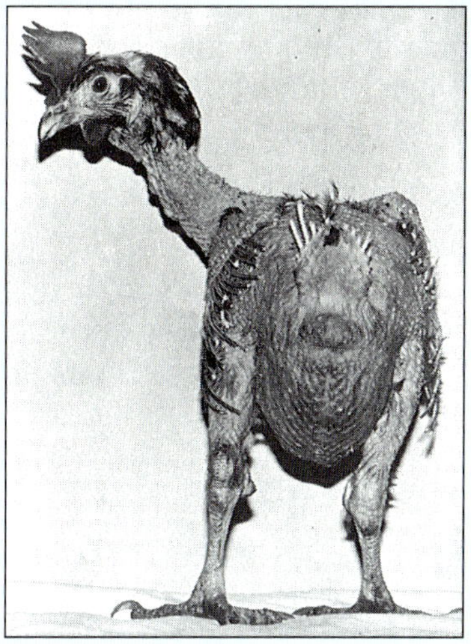

A battery hen

A *Discuss the advantages and disadvantages of keeping hens in batteries. Make a list of the main points raised.*

B *Why do the hens lay more eggs when they are kept in batteries?*

C *Research and find out how pigs, cattle or fish can be reared intensively. The school library may help.*

Questions and Activities

A Use the figures below to construct a pyramid of energy. The information in the **factfile** will help you. How much energy is lost from one square metre of grass when we eat beef?

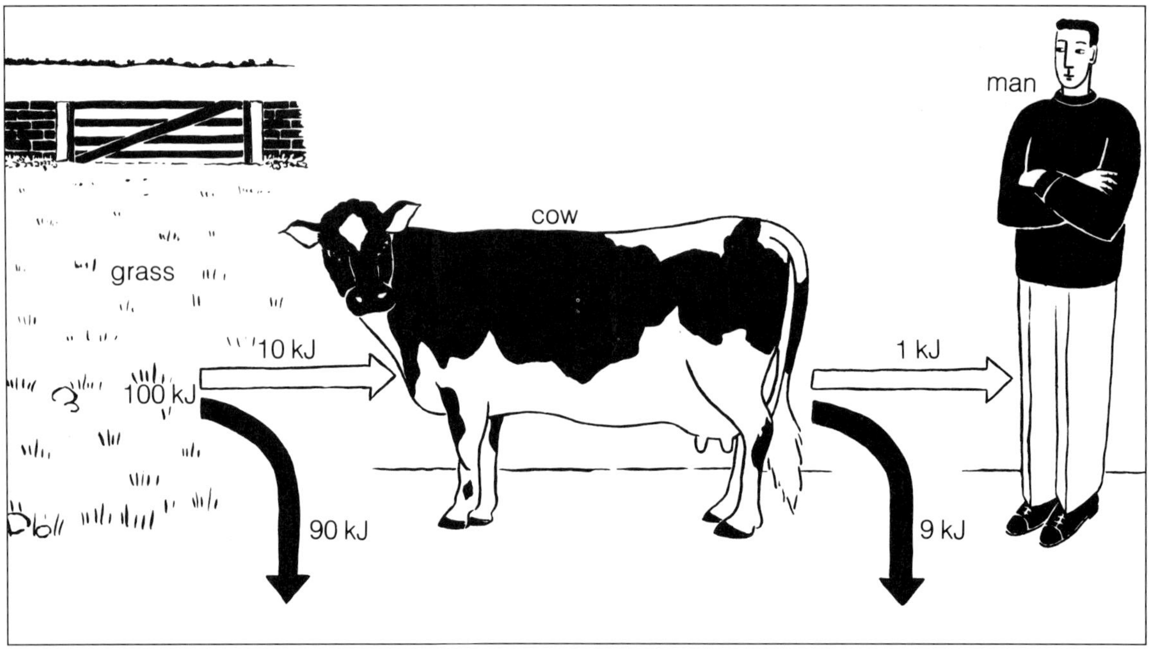

B Only part of the energy from food is used by the animals for growth. Write down other ways in which energy in food is used or lost.

C A lot of energy is lost when we eat beef from cattle reared in open fields. How can this loss be reduced by using modern intensive rearing methods?

D Your friend has written to you saying that he does not agree with you becoming a vegetarian. He says that if you were intended to live on grass alone, you would have been born with teeth and a digestion suited to eating grass.

Write a letter to your friend explaining your reasons for not eating meat. Use the ideas on page 24 to get you started.

E Mrs Roberts obtained these figures for the cows and sheep on her farm.

	sheep	cow
mass of grass consumed per day per animal	3 kg	70 kg
average total mass of animal	80 kg	600 kg
faeces per day per animal	1.2 kg	35 kg
urine per day per animal	1.3 l	20 l

- According to these figures which are better at converting grass into animal protein, cows or sheep?
- What happens to the remainder of the grass eaten by cows and sheep? Only some is passed out of the body as waste.

Ilkley Moor Baht'at

Read the words of the song 'Ilkley Moor Baht'at'

Where hast thou been since I saw thee?
On Ilkely Moor 'Baht'at
Where hast thou been since I saw thee?
Where hast thou been since I saw thee?
On Ilkely Moor 'Baht'at, on Ilkley Moor
'Baht'at, on Ilkely Moor 'Baht'at

I've been a courtin' Mary Jane
On Ilkely Moor 'Baht'at etc.

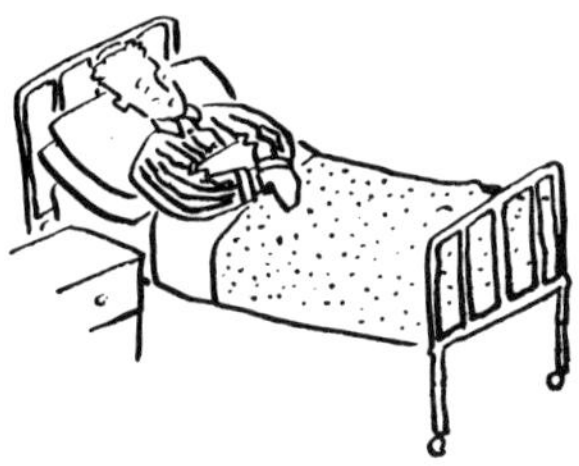

Thou'll go and get thee death o' cold
Then we shall have to bury thee
Then worms'll come and eat thee up
Then ducks'll come and eat up worms
Then we shall go and eat up the ducks
Then we will all have eaten thee
That's when we get our Irwin back

- Write down the food chain that it describes.

HUMAN → ________ → ________ → ____________

- Find out if this is a possible food chain.
- Could this be the answer to the world food shortage? Why is it not possible for one human body to provide sufficient chemical energy for another person to live on?
- Can you think of any other food chains which begin and end with the same organism?

KEEPING GOING

This bottle garden is a self-contained world of its own. It can carry on without anything being put in or taken out. The living things provide everything for each other.

A *Talk about the picture in small groups, or have a class discussion to discover what the plants give to the animals and what the animals give to the plants. Write a summary of your answers in your books.*

B *How is the bottle garden similar to the real world, and how is it different? Think about the way the plants and animals depend on each other. Present your answer as a list of similarities and a list of differences.*

ROTTEN TO THE CORE

The fact that things decay is often seen as a problem. We have to preserve food to stop it rotting. However, decay is a good thing in some ways.

A *Imagine a world where nothing ever rotted. Write a short article explaining what it would be like living in that world.*

B *Make a list of the advantages of decay. Can you think of any disadvantages?*

C *Which conditions affect the speed at which animals and plants decay?*

FACTFILE

KEEPING A BALANCE

GASES IN AIR

gas	percentage in air
nitrogen	approx. 80%
oxygen	approx. 20%
carbon dioxide	0.03%

RESPIRATION – GETTING ENERGY FROM FOOD

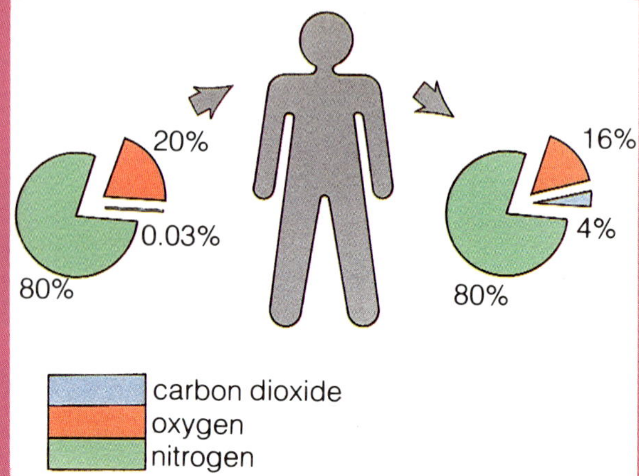

When animals breathe in and out, they change the air.

- *We make carbon dioxide inside us. The amount in the air we breathe rises from 0.03% (in) to 4% (out).*
- *We use up oxygen. The amount drops from 20% (in) to 16% (out).*
- *The amount of nitrogen does not change.*

The reaction which uses the oxygen and makes carbon dioxide is called **respiration**. *The purpose of respiration is to set free the energy in the food we have eaten. Then we can use the energy to move, to grow and to keep warm.*

THE EARTH'S ATMOSPHERE DOES NOT CHANGE

The Earth's atmosphere contains oxygen, carbon dioxide and nitrogen. From year to year the amount of each gas stays the same. This is true even though things are happening which could change the amounts.

Photosynthesis uses up carbon dioxide. *Plants use carbon dioxide to make food. They keep taking carbon dioxide from the air, but the supply never runs out.*

Respiration uses up oxygen. *Animals use up oxygen when they breathe. They never stop doing this as long as they live, but the air always stays fresh.*

RESPIRATION AND PHOTOSYNTHESIS – A BALANCING ACT

Green plants make food by **photosynthesis**. *Photosynthesis is the reverse of respiration. It uses carbon dioxide and produces oxygen.*

respiration photosynthesis

Respiration

food + oxygen → carbon dioxide + water + energy

$C_6H_{12}O_6 + 6O_2 \rightarrow 6CO_2 + 6H_2O + \text{energy}$

Photosynthesis

carbon dioxide + water + energy → food + oxygen

$6CO_2 + 6H_2O + \text{energy} \rightarrow C_6H_{12}O_6 + 6O_2$

MORE ABOUT CARBON DIOXIDE – ROTTING AND BURNING

Other processes use oxygen and make carbon dioxide in the same way as respiration.

Decay
Bacteria and fungi feed by rotting dead plants and animals. They get energy by doing this. They also decay waste such as faeces (animal droppings).

Burning
The energy is released as heat and light. The effect on the air is the same as respiration.

THE CARBON CYCLE

The same atoms of carbon are used over and over again.

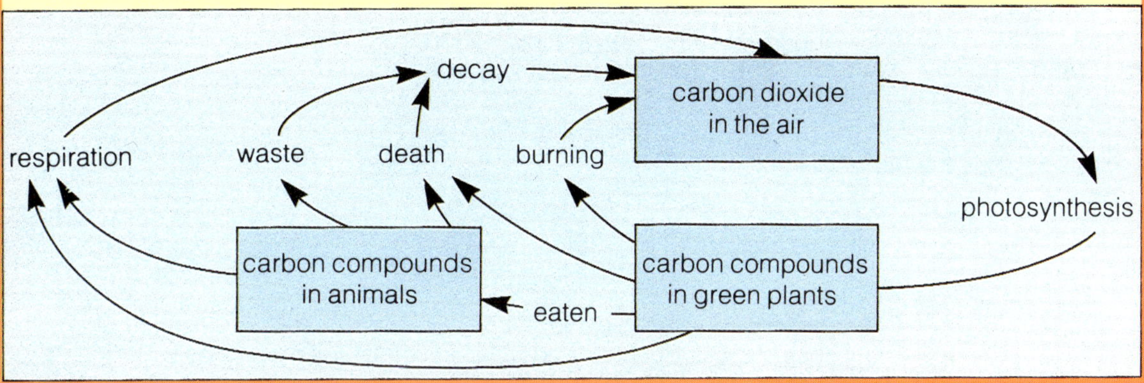

NITROGEN — ANOTHER ELEMENT WHICH IS RECYCLED

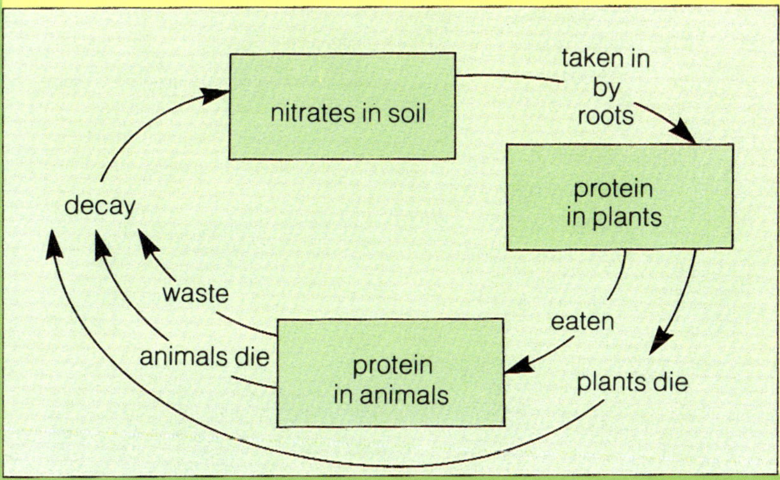

All living things need nitrogen. Proteins contain nitrogen, and we must have protein to live. Our muscles are made of protein.

Nitrogen is found dissolved in the soil in chemicals called nitrates. Plants take nitrogen in through their roots and use it to make protein.

The diagram shows the different things which could happen to the nitrogen before it ends up in the soil again. The atoms are used over and over again.

THE GREENHOUSE EFFECT

The amount of carbon dioxide in the atmosphere has been slowly rising for about 100 years. One prediction of the future pattern of carbon dioxide concentration is shown on the right. The level may double by the year 2040.

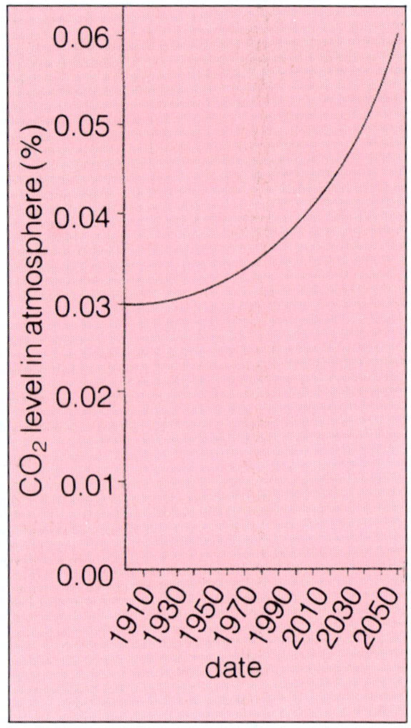

Why is the carbon dioxide increasing?

The balance of the carbon cycle has been spoiled. There are two parts to the problem. Industry is increasing all over the world. More fossil fuels are being burned than ever before, and this adds to the carbon dioxide in the air.

Photosynthesis is being cut back. The rainforests are being cleared for farmland. Seaweed and plankton are dying, killed by pollution.

Changing the climate

The carbon dioxide in the air acts as a blanket, stopping heat from escaping into space. This is called the **greenhouse effect** because the carbon dioxide acts in the same way as the panes of glass in a greenhouse. Energy enters as light and warms things up. Objects then give off the energy again, but in the form of heat. The heat waves cannot get out through the glass, so the greenhouse warms up. Some possible changes in climate are shown in the table below.

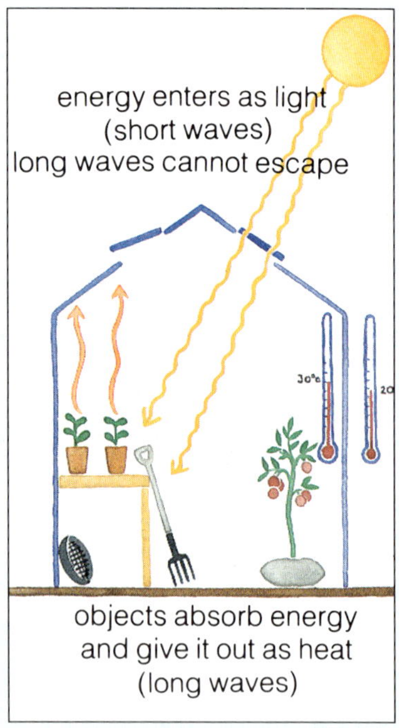

Doubling the carbon dioxide could warm the Earth by 2 or 3 degrees centigrade

area	change in climate	other changes
North America and Canada	Warmer and drier. Droughts from time to time.	Less food produced. Loss of grain surplus – none left over to feed the Third World.
Europe and North Africa	Warmer and wetter because of extra evaporation from the seas. Possible flooding.	More food produced. This may take some time to happen.
Polar ice caps	Warmer	Some melting. Sea levels could rise by up to 6 metres. Floods in lowlands.

A *Collect newspaper cuttings about weather around the world. Also watch out for reports on television. Are there any signs that the climate really is changing?*

B *Write a summary of your findings in the form of a newspaper article.*

BACK TO THE SOIL

Humans break the nitrogen cycle by farming. The nitrogen is taken from the soil in our crops, but does not go back again afterwards. It ends up in the sewers instead, as urine and faeces.

Eventually the soil will become exhausted, and no more crops will grow. There are a number of ways of solving this problem.

- Sewage works use filters and bacteria tanks to turn sewage into **sludge** which can safely go back to the fields.
- Artificial nitrate fertilizer can be made in factories using nitrogen from the air.
- Nitrogen-fixing bacteria make nitrates from atmospheric nitrogen. Plants with the bacteria in their roots can be planted to improve the soil. Clover, peas and beans are all useful for this.

Bean root nodules contain nitrogen fixing bacteria

The best source of natural fertilizer

These purification ponds handle waste water from agroindustry in Southern Thailand

Danger – plants feeding!

Soil sometimes contains too little nitrogen for plants to grow properly.

Insectivorous plants can catch and digest insects. They take nitrogen compounds from the bodies of the insects. They can survive where other plants cannot.

The Venus Flytrap lives in damp bogs in North Carolina, USA

The Asian pitcher plant has nectar round the rim and is slippery inside

A *Bacteria and fungi cause decay. Flies, maggots and other insects all help. List the reasons why decomposers are so important. Think about the nitrogen and carbon cycles.*

B *Make a large copy of the nitrogen cycle from page 31. Use the information on this page to add more parts to it, so that it tells the whole story of the way nitrogen atoms are recycled.*

Questions and Activities

A Copy the paragraph and use the words in the list to fill in the blank spaces. You can use some words twice.

respiration, carbon dioxide, food, energy, oxygen, photosynthesis

When animals breathe they change the air. They use up some of the ______ and breathe out extra ______. The oxygen is used in a chemical reaction called ______. The reason they do this is to get ______ from food. Green plants respire too, but they can also do something which is the reverse. It is called ______. This reaction balances respiration because it uses up ______ and makes ______. The plant does it to make ______.

B Look back in this book to page 28. Predict what would happen if there were many more snails in the bottle garden, say about twenty. Give the reasons for your answer.

C A river, polluted by sewage, becomes choked with fungi and bacteria. All of the green plants and animals may die. Explain why this happens.

The polluted estuary of the River Miera near Santander, Spain

D List the advantages of spreading cow dung on fields.

E When a forest is first cleared the land gives good crops to begin with. After a few years the yield is less, and in the end nothing will grow.

- Explain how the original forest kept growing without exhausting the soil.
- Why does taking crops *spoil* the earth?
- Make a list of the things a farmer could do to keep the soil fertile.

F This is the Fly Agaric – it is a poisonous fungus. Unlike green plants fungi can live in very shady parts of a wood. They will even grow in complete darkness.

Answer these questions in your notebooks. Give a clear explanation.

- Why do green plants need the light?
- How does the fungus get the energy it needs to live?
- How is this fungus helping the green plants growing nearby?

Cooling off

Here are some things that have been suggested to help cope with the greenhouse effect problem.

- Stop burning coal, oil and gas. Change to nuclear power for electricity supplies.
- Ban the clearing of forest in South America. Plant new forest wherever possible.
- Just let it happen. Abandon any land which floods, or build up sea walls to hold back the sea.

Imagine what the following people would have to say about those ideas.

A poor farmer in Brazil who wants more land to grow crops for his family

An executive of British Coal

A member of a protest group which is trying to prevent a nuclear power station being built locally

A senior politician in Holland, most of which is at or below sea level

- Write a summary of the views of each person.
- Produce a report for the United Nations suggesting actions which could be taken to reduce the greenhouse effect.
- What can you do in your own life to help? Write down three things you could do. Explain how they would help.

THE SEAL IN DANGER

The grey seal is a creature which always seems to be in the news. Recently there have been two main stories in the press.

Claims that there were *too many* seals in Canandian waters led to large numbers being killed by hunters. This caused a great public outcry.

More recently a fatal disease similar to pneumonia killed huge numbers of seals in the North Sea. Now people worry that there may be *too few*!

It seems that the seal just cannot win. Seals are beautiful animals, and it is always sad to see animals suffering. We would want to help them just for that reason. Is there more to it? Are the problems of the seal a sign of something going wrong which could become a problem for human beings?

A dead grey seal

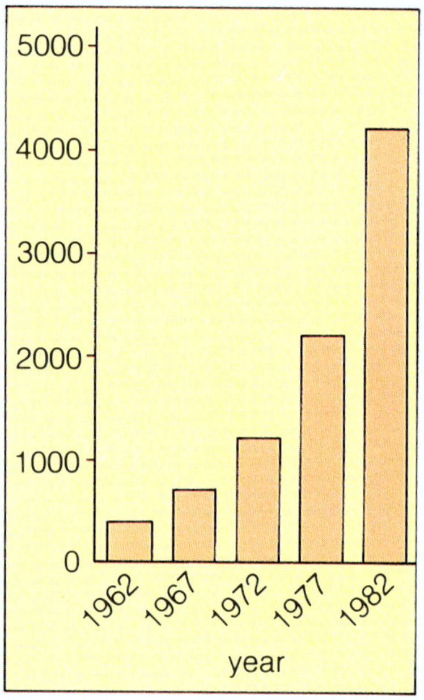

Sable Island is in the Arctic waters of Canada. The seals were increasing by about 13% each year. In Britain the rate of increase was about 7% a year

Epidemic

In 1988 it became clear that the seal population in European seas was in serious trouble. Hundreds of dead and dying seals were washed ashore. A virus disease similar to distemper, a common illness in dogs, was found to be the cause.

Nobody was quite sure why the seals were suddenly being killed by this disease. The North Sea is badly polluted with sewage and waste from factories. Perhaps this had made the seals too weak to fight the disease. Overcrowding lets any illness spread more quickly and perhaps the population of seals really had grown too large.

The Arctic food web

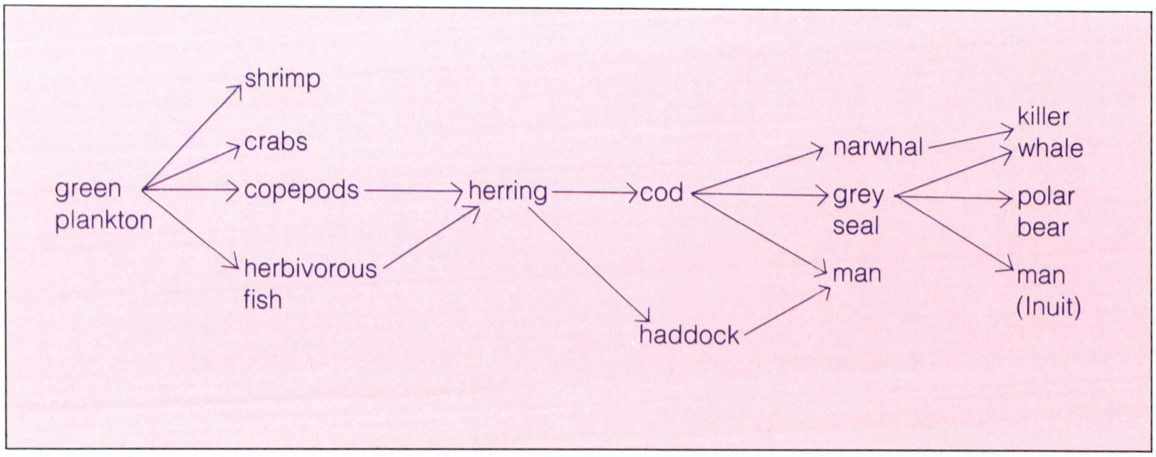

The opinions

These two imaginary articles do show real opinions.

The Comet

Don't let me die

FUR TRADERS IN NEW SEAL MASSACRE

Once again the snows of Northern Canada are red with the blood of baby seals. The butchers of the Northern wastes are at it again.
Our reporter saw the sickening sight of hundreds of baby seals killed in front of their mothers; clubbed to avoid making bullet holes in the valuable pelts. The rewards are huge. Rich women pay hundreds of dollars for a fur coat made from innocent baby seals.

CAMPAIGN
Help "The Comet" stamp out this disgusting bloodbath. Write to your MP today. We are looking for **ONE MILLION** letters. Write today and save a seal!

Reporter: *You have just returned from killing seal pups. World opinion is against you. Why do you do it?*

Fisherman: We don't like to do it, but we have to make a living.

Reporter: *But your proper job is fishing. Why kill seals?*

Fisherman: Because they eat the fish we need to catch. There are too many seals these days. The cod they take could be feeding people!

Reporter: *Are you telling me that you don't sell the coats to fur traders?*

Fisherman: We do, but why not? We would still have to kill the seals even if we didn't sell the skins.

A *Write the letter which 'The Comet' asks you to send to your MP.*

- *You might support a ban on seal culling, or you might take the opposite view.*
- *Whatever you think, you should explain your reasons very clearly. Your MP will only do something if you can make out a good case.*

B *Seals are endangered in two ways. The epidemic may wipe them out. If they recover the hunting may start again.*

- *Use the food web to predict the effect on other members of the web, including man, if seals become extinct.*
- *Suggest some natural factors which might have controlled the population.*
- *Is it right for man to decide how many seals there should be?*

THE STORY OF DDT

DAILY NEWS
24th March 1942

DDT KILLS ALL INSECTS

A new insecticide has been developed which kills all known insects. Scientists believe that it has no harmful affects on other animals.

NEW YORK TIMES
5th May 1952

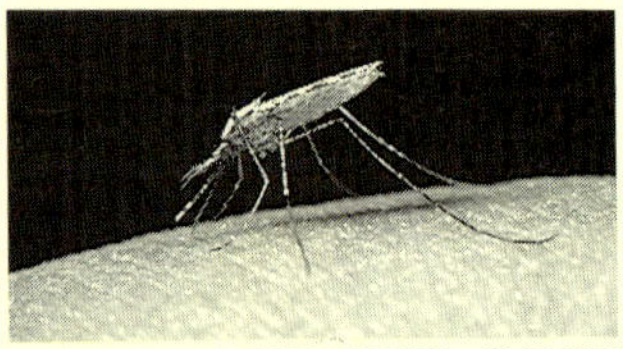

DDT WIPES OUT MALARIA

Malaria has been virtually eliminated thanks to DDT. The mosquitoes which carried Malaria have been killed by spraying all the marshy areas where their larval stages developed with DDT.

Wild Life April 1953

Birds of prey are dying

It has been reported that many birds of prey are dying. These include eagles, ospreys and peregrine falcons. Experts are puzzled by the cause of death.

EAGLES IN DANGER

Many eagles and other birds of prey are failing to breed. They lay eggs but these do not hatch.

Use of DDT Banned in US and parts of Europe

PENGUINS CONTAIN DDT

Scientists are alarmed by the presence of DDT in tissues of penguins. Those examined were from Antarctica. DDT has never been used in this country. It is not clear how this chemical could have got into their bodies.

FOOD CHAIN CONCENTRATES DDT

Scientists made some important discoveries when they investigated the DDT content of the animals in an American lake. Small shrimps feed on organic matter in the mud at the bottom. The shrimps are eaten by fish and these are eaten by herring gulls. They carried out measurements of the DDT levels in the mud and the animals in the food chain.

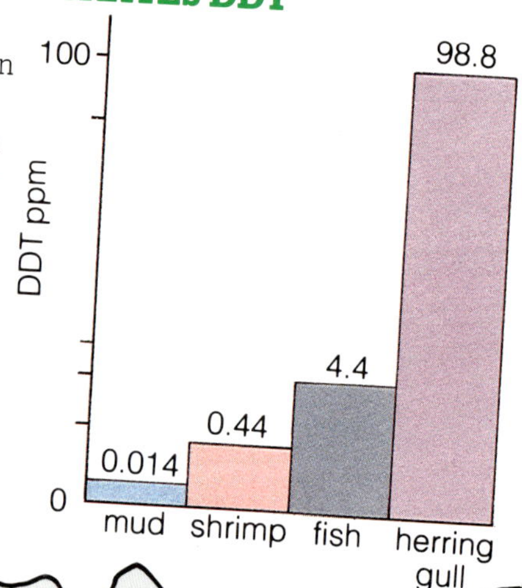

IS BREAST MILK SAFE FOR BABIES?

Babies may be in danger from breast milk. This was the alarming news when levels of DDT were found to be four times higher in mother's milk than the allowed limit for cow's milk. How dangerous DDT is to humans is still uncertain.

Wild Life JUNE 1974

DDT Kills

Scientists have now been able to show that DDT affects the female bird. It upsets the balance of hormones that is essential to the uptake of calcium needed for strong egg-shells. The bird continues to lay eggs as normal but the shells are too thin to protect the embryo inside. In some cases eggs have been found with no shells at all.

The pesticide food chain

Do we need pesticides?

To obtain maximum yield of food we grow single crops over large areas of land. Under these conditions pests are far more likely to spread quickly and cause serious damage to the crops. The use of pesticides will prevent this happening.

There are safer pesticides now. Unlike DDT some will break down naturally a few days after use. This avoids the build up of toxic chemicals in the tissues of animals at the end of the food chain.

Without using pesticides far more people in the world would die of starvation.

The numbers of barn-owls have been decreasing in the last few years. It is believed that changes in the pesticides used to control rats and mice may be partly responsible.

Pesticides in water cause death or deformities to the tadpoles of frogs and toads reducing their numbers.

Widespread use of insecticides has reduced dramatically the numbers of butterflies. Many are now threatened with extinction.

No one is sure of the long term effects to us when we eat food containing pesticides.

Wildlife is still being destroyed by the use of pesticides.

A *Look at the food chain in the illustration and answer the questions below.*

- *How did the DDT get into the gnat larvae?*
- *Explain why there is more DDT in the heron tissue than in the gnat larvae.*
- *If a new pesticide is developed, choose those characteristics from the list below that would be useful:*

  long lasting;
  breaks down rapidly after use;
  kills a large number of different animals;
  specific for one animal only;
  non-toxic to plants;
  kills weeds as well.

B *Pesticides are fairly cheap. Farmers using them are able to grow more crops. These chemicals can cause serious damage to wildlife and maybe to humans. If you were the Minister of the Environment and had to make plans for the future, what would you do? Include in your plans the reasons for your decisions.*

C *Design an advertisement for a pesticide to appear in a farmer's magazine.*

OR

D *Design a poster for a conservation group which draws attention to one of the problems of using pesticides.*

THE GOLDEN EAGLE

Ian was excited. What a find! He knew his father had kept a diary about eagles but who could this have belonged to?

There must have been lots of eagles around when it was written. Maybe he might see one. He had heard there was an eagle's nest nearby.

There it was! A male golden eagle. Ian watched as it swooped towards a young hare. The dead hare was carried high and then dropped into the eyrie.

It had been a difficult climb. Ian saw the larger eaglet pushing the smaller one away and then turning back to feed on the pieces of hare.

Ian looked up. The eagle had flown above him as he climbed down the rocks. It turned and swooped. Ian ducked. He could feel the rush of air as it went past.

Ian felt pleased with himself. He looked again at the diary his father had kept. Now he would be able to keep his own records.

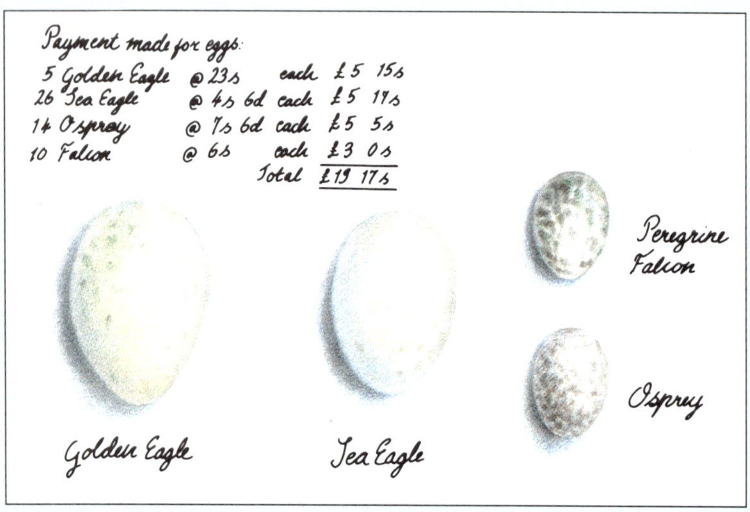

Payment made for eggs:

5 Golden Eagle	@ 23s	each	£5 15s
26 Sea Eagle	@ 4s 6d	each	£5 17s
14 Osprey	@ 7s 6d	each	£5 5s
10 Falcon	@ 6s	each	£3 0s
		Total	£19 17s

Part of record book found in attic dated 1837

An eagle in flight

Facts about eagles

- In the 1800s eggs were collected by naturalists. Birds were killed and stuffed to add to their collections.
- Sea eagles were more common than golden eagles. Now sea eagles no longer breed in Britain.
- For many years hill sheep farmers killed eagles believing they were responsible for taking lambs.
- Gamekeepers poisoned or shot eagles to protect grouse.
- Eagles are known to feed on carrion, particularly dead sheep.
- During the 1960s many eagles failed to rear young.
- Addled eggs when examined contained residues of chemicals used in sheep dips. These chemicals have since been banned.
- The eagle is now a protected bird. You cannot visit eyries without a licence. It is an offence to take, kill or injure an eagle; to take, damage or disturb its eggs or young.

The young are fed by their parents for three months before they can hunt for themselves. The parent bird is shown returning with a leafy twig used to decorate the nest

2 APRIL VISITED TREETOPS. FOUND NEW EYRIE WITH TWO EGGS. THAT MAKES THREE NESTS WITH EGGS.

7 MAY TWO HAVE HATCHED AT HIGH POINT. THEY LOOK FANTASTIC.

8 MAY ONE EGG HAS HATCHED AT TREETOPS. I THINK THE OTHER ONE IS ADDLED.

14 MAY BOTH EAGLETS ALIVE AT HIGH POINT. ONE LOOKS VERY WEAK. I DON'T THINK IT WILL SURVIVE.

15 MAY NEITHER OF THE EGGS AT CRAG SIDE HAVE HATCHED. FEMALE HAS LEFT.

18 MAY MISSED SCHOOL TODAY. ONLY ONE EAGLET AT HIGH POINT BUT IT SEEMS TO BE GROWING FAST.

10 JULY I HAVE NOT BEEN ABLE TO VISIT THE EYRIES FOR A LONG TIME. EAGLET FROM HIGH POINT HAS ALREADY FLOWN. THE EAGLET AT TREETOPS LOOKS READY TO FLY.

Page from father's diary dated 1966

YEAR	SITE	NUMBER OF EGGS	NUMBER HATCHED	NUMBER REARED
1964	1	2	2	1
	2	2	0	0
	3	0	0	0
1965	1	1	0	0
	2	2	2	1
	3	2	2	0
1966	1	2	2	1
	2	2	2	0
	3	2	1	1

Summary of records for three years

A *Why did Ian think that eagles were more common in the 1800s?*

B *Look at his father's diary. What were the names of sites 1, 2 and 3?*

C *Give reasons for the numbers of eagles falling during the 1800s?*

D *When did the numbers fall even more drastically? What caused this?*

E *In the last few years the numbers have been increasing again. Suggest reasons for this happening.*

F *What must we do to ensure that the number of eagles continues to increase?*

G *Design a poster giving advice on how to protect the golden eagle.*

CASE STUDY FOUR

ETHIOPIA – COLLAPSE OF AN ENVIRONMENT

The environment in parts of Africa seems to be collapsing. It has never been easy living next to the Sahara desert; Ethiopia has had famines for hundreds of years. Now the problem has got much worse very quickly.

- A fifth less food is grown now than in 1960.
- Rainfall is less than half of the normal amount. Some parts now have almost none at all.
- Areas once green with forest or farmland are now dry and unused.

We must learn how to prevent this kind of disaster. The people of Ethiopia are as capable and hard working as anyone else in the world. Something has happened to spoil their land. It would be foolish to think that the same could never happen in Europe.

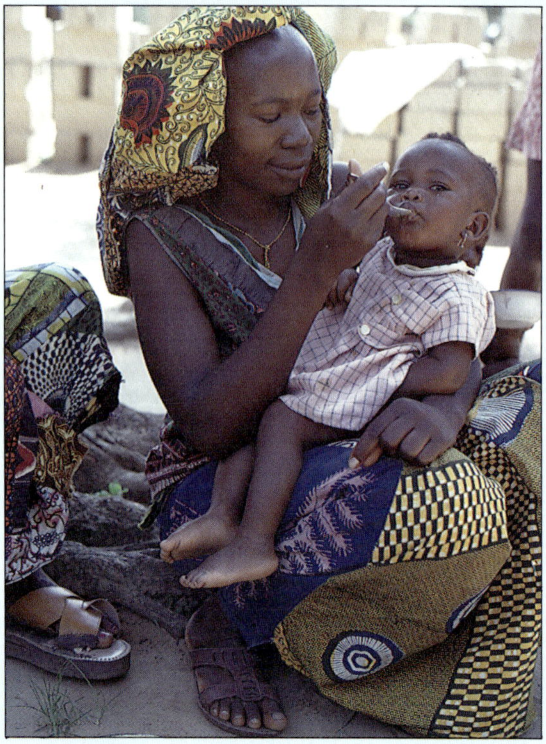

This child is one of the lucky ones

The Sahel

The area most in danger is called the Sahel. It lies between the Sahara desert and tropical Africa. The climate is dry and hot, but crops could be grown before the rains failed. Animals grazed on the sparse scrubland and grass.

The Sahel is huge. Ethiopia alone is five times the size of the United Kingdom. On the map you can see the other countries which are affected. 80 million people live in the threatened countries. In the 1985 drought ten million had to leave their homes to find food.

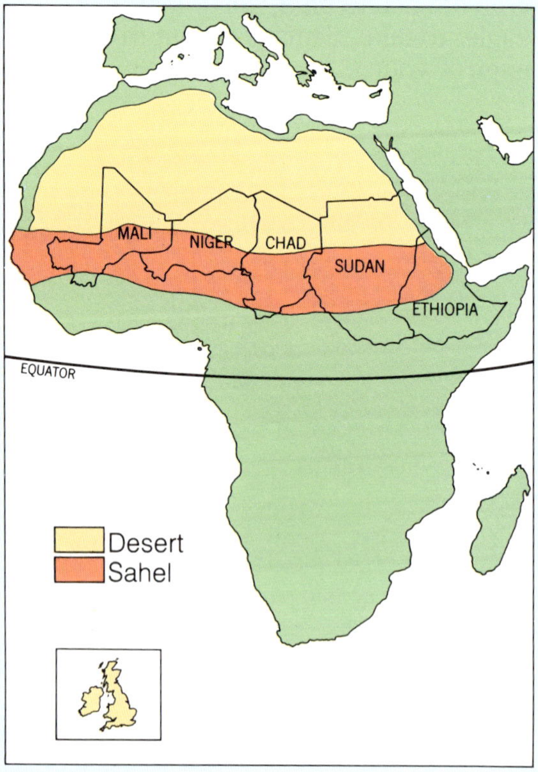

The area affected is huge. Britain is shown drawn to the same scale

From 1980 the July rains began to fail. By 1985 crisis point had been reached. Food stocks were gone – even the grain kept back for planting had been eaten. Farm animals had died. The great movement to the relief camps began.

Why did the rains fail? Why had food stocks got so low? Several different things had been adding up for many years until finally the whole environment was ruined.

What caused the drought in Ethiopia?

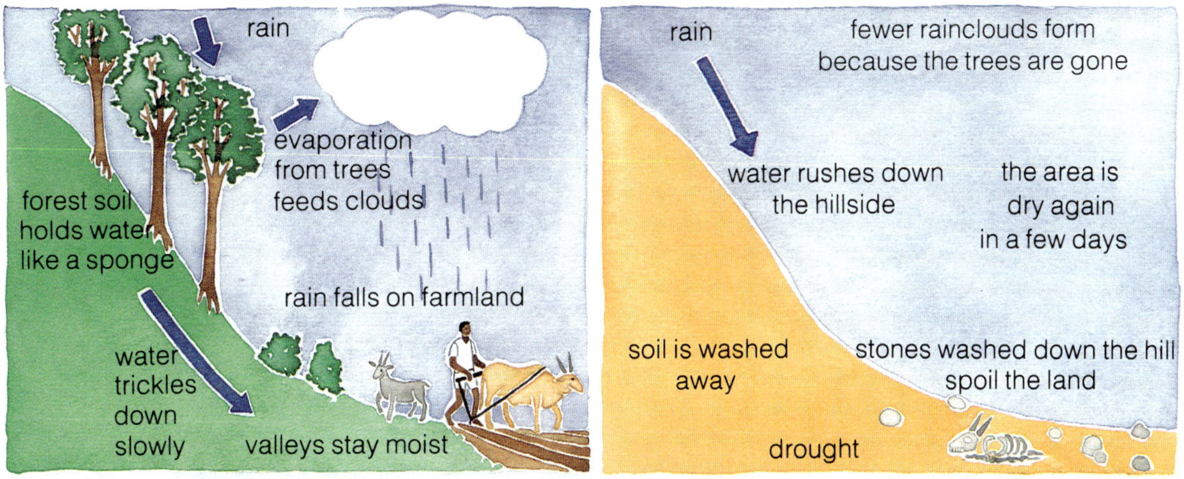

Forests have been cleared 80 years ago Ethiopia was almost half covered with forest. Now it has nearly all gone. The growing population cleared the forests for farmland and firewood. This set off two of the main parts of the disaster – soil erosion and a drop in rainfall.

Cow dung is burned for fuel Firewood is hard to find now the forests are gone. Having to burn the dung means it can't be used as fertilizer – so fewer crops grow.

The Sahara desert is growing Every year the desert moves 100 m further south into the Sahel. This loss of land puts more strain on the parts that are left.

Foreign debt Ethiopia owes money to foreign banks. To pay it off cash crops such as coffee are grown. This uses up land which could grow food.

War All through the crisis, wars inside Ethiopia have used up money and manpower. It makes it difficult to move food supplies.

Poor roads Some parts of the country are hundreds of miles from a good road. Moving food supplies is almost impossible.

Locusts Swarms of locusts attack the crops. Controlling them is difficult because of all the other problems.

A *Bangladesh has been suffering from floods. They have been blamed on deforestation.*

- *Find out more about the floods in Bangladesh and explain how loss of forest causes flooding. Use diagrams like the ones on this page.*

B *Could a problem as big as this ever happen in Britain? Collect newspaper and magazine articles about damage to the environment in Britain, and make a display in your classroom.*

C *You have probably had the chance to help raise money for Ethiopia. Here are some of the things that aid from the West has been spent on.*

Lorries, fuel, spare parts, seeds, airlifts of food, fertilizer, planting forest, locust control, medicines, tents, soil protection, irrigation, farming tools, agriculture training, drilling machinery for wells, food supplies, clothing and blankets.

- *Sort these into two lists headed* emergency relief *and* long term development*.*
- *Pick the project from the list which you think is the most important, and explain your choice to the class.*

Crops and climate

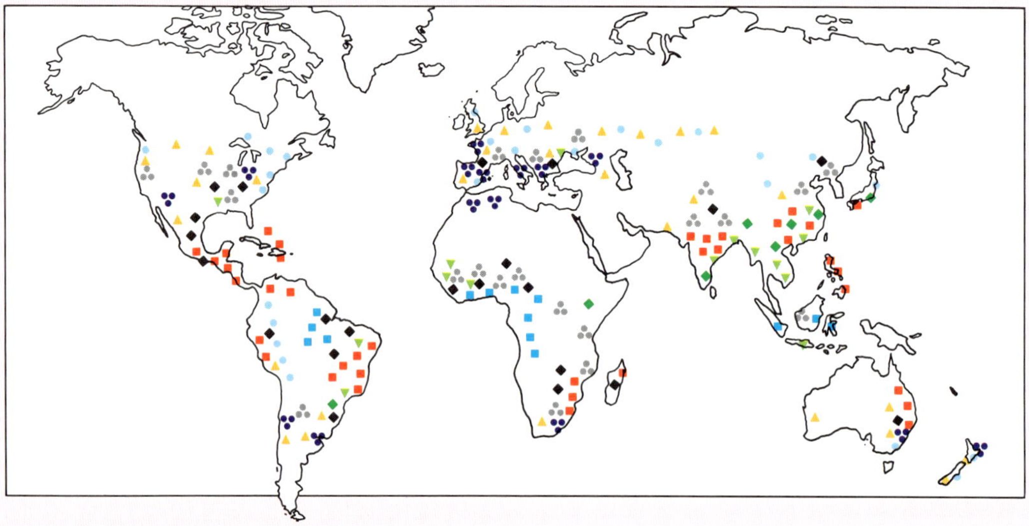

Rice is grown mainly in the monsoon belt. It needs warm conditions where heavy seasonal rains allow the farmers to flood large areas of soil to a depth of one metre or more. The crop takes about 25 weeks from seed to harvesting.

Wheat is the most important food crop in the temperate zone. It grows best in regions that receive less than 750 mm of rain a year. It requires a short cold season during the early stages of its growth to discourage diseases.

Millet is a cereal which can grow in dryer warmer regions. It is the leading grain of Africa and is also grown in other countries such as India, Pakistan, China and the United States.

Maize grown in tropical regions is sown in the wet season to ripen in the dry season. In the temperate zone it is planted in the spring and harvested in the autumn. Maize is killed by frost and needs 85 frost-free days after planting.

Sugar cane is a giant grass which is harvested before it produces seed. It is easy to grow. It needs a rich, deep well-drained soil with a hot moist climate and a rainfall of about 1500 mm a year.

Potatoes originally grew wild in the Andean mountains of Peru. Here the potato grew well in the cool damp environment at high altitudes. This is why it thrives in the temperate zones of North America and Europe.

Tea is an evergreen bush. It is a hardy plant and can stand frost but it grows rapidly only in hot countries with a heavy rainfall. Under a monsoon climate it produces fresh, green leaves in each rainy spell. These are dried before use.

Grapes are used for making wine. The vines grow well in warm, sunny climates. They need an average temperature of 16°C and in the spring some rain and no frost. Moist conditions in the summer cause the fruit to rot.

Rubber trees need constant heat and a high rainfall. Each tree has special channels which contain a white, milky fluid called latex. When the tree is damaged the latex flows out. Heating with sulphur produces the rubber.

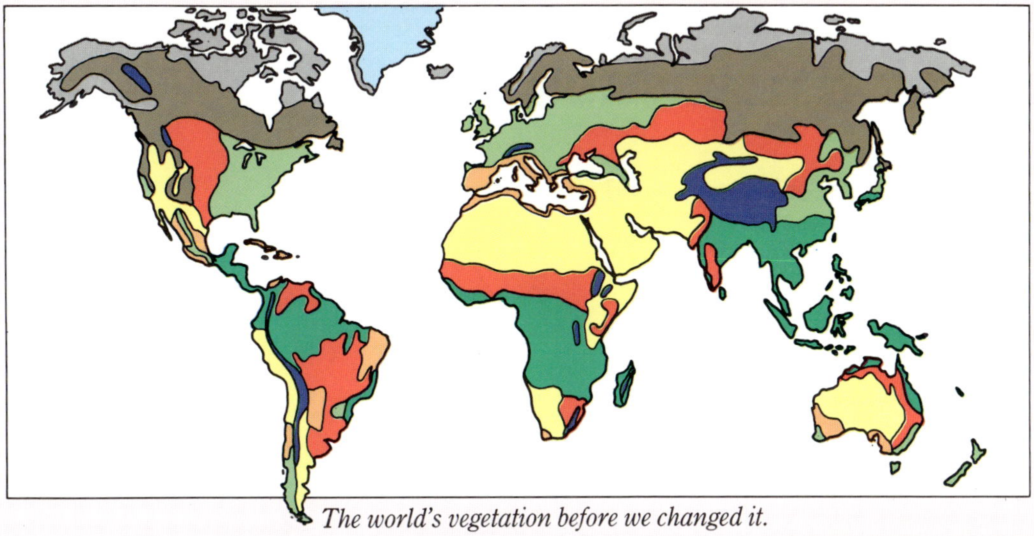

The world's vegetation before we changed it.

Permanent ice Very cold, dry permanent ice cover. No vegetation.

Tundra Short summers, cold winters, 9 months below 5°C.

Deciduous forest Cool summers, mild wet winters. 1–5 months below 5°C. Grey/brown soils rich in nutrients.

Coniferous forest Short summers, cold winters. 6–9 months below 5°C. Acid, grey soils which contain little humus.

Mountains The vegetation changes with altitude.

Mediterranean Warm/hot dry summers, warm fairly dry winters. Scrubland, drought resistant small trees and bushes.

Grassland/savanna Hot wet summers, hot dry winters. Grasses and scattered trees. Fertile brown and black soils.

Desert/semi-desert Hot dry summers, warm dry winters. Very little vegetation or grasses and drought resistant shrubs.

Tropical rain forest Hot and wet all year. Evergreen trees growing all year. Poor red soils low in nutrients.

Extension Activities

A The population of people on an island has been increasing. They are no longer able to produce sufficient food to feed themselves.

- Redraw the pie chart showing how the islanders could change the use of the land to feed more people.
- Explain the advantages and disadvantages of your scheme.

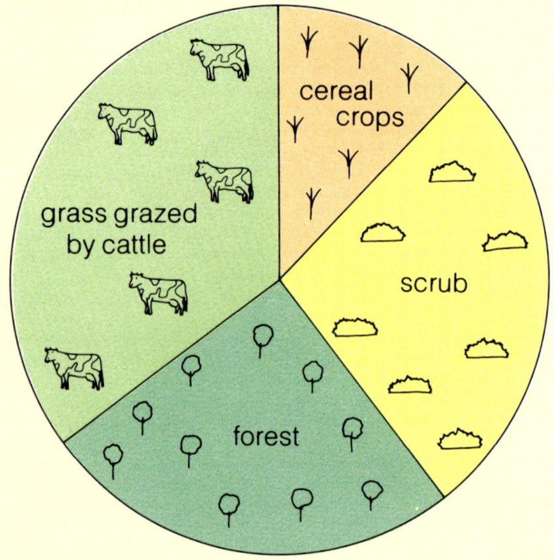

Land cover of island

B Study the statements in the grid. Some may be used to support the argument that tropical rain forests should be cleared. Others show why the rain forests need to be preserved.

After replanting it takes several hundred years for a tropical rain forest to grow.	Soil washed into rivers causes them to silt up. This increases the chances of flooding.	Demand for tropical wood has increased from 109 million m^3 in 1973 to 145 million m^3 in 1980 to 215 million m^3 in 1990.
Trees remove carbon dioxide from the air and release oxygen.	Bangladesh has four times as much flooding now compared with 25 years ago.	Felled timber is needed for firewood.
Many rare species of plants and animals are found in rain forests.	Extra farmland is needed to produce food for the rapidly growing population.	Rare wildlife is being preserved in nature reserves.
Sale of timber provides much needed money.	Oil, gas and coal are expensive forms of fuel.	Forest clearance leads to soil erosion.

- First sort them into two groups; those which support cutting down rain forests and those which support their preservation.
- Prepare two different reports from this information. One report should explain why it is important to stop cutting down the rain forests. The other should report the view that the removal of the rain forest has to continue.

C Choose a way to display these results as graphs. Your graphs should help you compare the different temperatures and rainfalls of the five places for each month.

	A		B		C		D		E	
	mm	°C	mm	°C	mm	°C	mm	°C	mm	°C
J	250	26	0	24	0	22	25	−28	50	10
F	175	27	0	26	0	23	20	−22	40	12
M	195	27	0	31	7	27	15	−19	32	13
A	184	28	0	35	0	32	15	0	20	15
M	175	27	18	36	10	36	25	8	18	19
J	175	27	105	33	25	34	27	14	17	24
J	172	27	210	28	80	34	30	15	10	26
A	200	27	210	27	48	33	30	12	15	26
S	180	27	140	27	20	33	28	6	17	23
O	210	27	50	29	18	32	26	− 4	50	18
N	252	27	10	28	0	27	25	−17	75	13
D	254	27	5	25	0	24	24	−27	63	12

- Describe the seasonal variation for each place. The following details will make your description more accurate:

  minimum temperature;
  maximum temperature;
  annual temperature range (lowest to highest);
  annual rainfall (total in mm);
  rainfall distribution (e.g. wet summer, dry winter).

- Suggest where each place may be.
- What type of vegetation would you expect to find in each region if it had not been changed by farming?
- Suggest how each of these places could be used for food production or alternative cash crops. What changes would need to take place to make the land more productive?
- Draw graphs to show the pattern of results you would expect for rainfall and temperature in New Zealand.

D Records were kept for 10 years of numbers of antelopes and lions in a National Park. The lions fed mainly on the antelopes. The changes in their populations are shown in the graph.

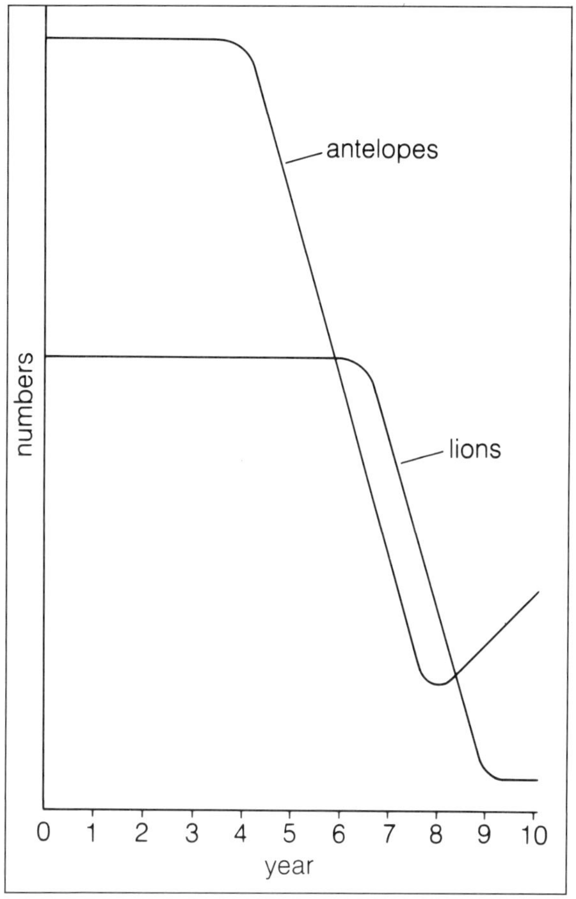

- Describe the changes in the antelope population from years 1 to 10.
- Suggest three possible reasons why the number of antelopes decreased.
- Why do you think the lion numbers decreased?
- What would you expect to happen for the next five years to the numbers of lions and antelopes?

Index

Algae 8
Alpine 6
Ashwoods 4, 5
Asian pitcher plant 33

Bacteria 31, 33
Balance 30, 31
Barn-owl 16, 17
Battery hens 25
Beechwoods 4, 5
Bluebells 6
Bottle garden 28
Breeding 15, 16
Burning 31

Carbon cycle 31
Carbon dioxide 22, 23, 30, 31, 32
Carnivore 14, 15, 23
Cellulose 22
Chlorophyll 21, 22, 23
Chloroplasts 21
Climate 32, 44, 45
Clover 7, 33
Coniferous forest 45
Community 13, 15
Competition 17
Courtship 16
Cow dung 43
Crops 44

DDT 38, 39
Death 31
Decay 29, 31
Deforestation 43, 46
Desert 42, 45, 46
Diving beetle 13
Drought 17, 42

Eagles 40, 41
Earth's atmosphere 30
Eggs 16, 25, 40, 41
Energy 23, 30, 31, 32
Energy chains 23
Energy pyramids 23
Environments 4, 5, 6, 7, 13, 16, 17, 28, 33
Ethiopia 42
Exhaled air 30

Factory farming 24
Fertilizers 8, 9, 24, 33
Fishing 37
Food 12, 13, 14, 15, 16, 44
Food chains 12, 14, 17
Food webs 13, 15, 36
Forests 43, 45
Fungi 31
Fur coats 37
Gases in the air 30
Green leaves 21, 22, 23
Greenhouse effect 32
Grey seals 37

Habitats 4, 5, 8, 9, 15, 16, 28
Heavy soil 7
Herbicides 8, 9
Heron 13, 39

Inhaled air 30
Insecticides 38, 39

Kingfisher 13

Larvae 13, 38
Light levels 6
Light soil 7
Limiting factors 15
Locusts 43
Loss of habitat 17

Malaria 38
Marshes 8
Mass pyramids 23
Mayfly larvae 13
Meadows 8, 9
Mediterranean 44, 45
Mosquito 13, 38

Nesting sites 16
Nitrates 8, 31
Nitrogen 7, 31
Number pyramids 23
Nutrients 7

Old man's beard 6
Omnivore 15
Osprey 38, 40, 41
Otter 9
Oxygen 22, 30

Penguin 38
Perch 13
Peregrine falcon 38, 40, 41
Pesticides 17, 38, 39
pH 6
Phloem 21
Phosphorus 7, 8
Photosynthesis 21, 22, 23, 30, 32
Pitfall trap 14
Plankton 32
Plant breeding 24
Pond life 13
Populations 14, 15
Potassium 7, 8
Predator 15
Prickly pear 6
Proteins 22, 31
Protozoa 13

Quinine 38

Respiration 30, 31
Rhododendron 6
Rotting 29, 31

Sable Island 36
Sahara desert 42, 43
Sahel 42
Savannah 45
Seal culling 37, 38
Seaweed 32
Sewage works 33
Snow cover 17
Soil texture 7
Species 15
Starch 22
Stomata 21
Sugar factory 20
Sugars 20, 21, 22, 23

Tadpoles 13, 39
Temperature 6
Test for starch 22
Tropical rain forest 45, 46

Venus fly trap 33

Weather conditions 44, 45